Fear

Contents

Fear

by David Orme

Ransom

Trailblazers

Fear
by David Orme
Educational consultant: Helen Bird

Illustrated by Ulises Roman

Published by Ransom Publishing Ltd.
51 Southgate Street, Winchester, Hants. SO23 9EH
www.ransom.co.uk

ISBN   978 184167 805 4

First published in 2009

2

Fear

Get the facts

What are you frightened of?

Are you frightened of ...

Spiders?

Little spiders are sometimes called **money-spiders**. They are supposed to bring **good luck**.

This **bird-eating spider** might frighten you – but it would frighten some birds more!

Snakes?

This one might frighten you.

Anacondas have eaten people. They swallow their prey whole.

But this is even more scary. Its bite will kill very quickly.

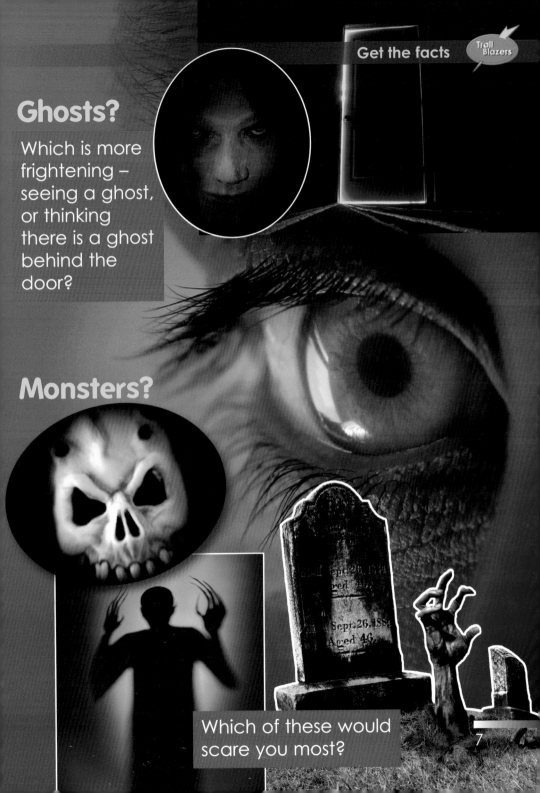

Ghosts?

Which is more frightening – seeing a ghost, or thinking there is a ghost behind the door?

Monsters?

Which of these would scare you most?

Is fear always bad?

Being scared isn't always bad.

- It's a good thing to be afraid of heights.

- We need to be afraid of fire.

8

Fear is a **warning** – it tells us that something might be dangerous.

When we feel we are in **danger**, **blood** is pumped to our **muscles** to get the body ready to fight – or run away.

This is called **fight or flight**.

Sometimes we are frightened just because something is **unexpected**. That's because our bodies need to react instantly – to be ready for danger without stopping to think.

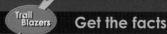
Phobias

Sometimes people are terrified by one special thing.

If this seriously affects their life, it is called a phobia.

Some people have a phobia about **planes**.

They don't like flying.

Having a phobia about **insects** means it is impossible to go outside unless you are totally covered up.

Some people won't leave their house. They have a phobia about **open spaces**.

Other people have a phobia about **being trapped in a small space**.

People can develop phobias about all sorts of things.

It may seem funny that people can be frightened of **clowns**, or **birds**, or **cats**, but these fears can have a terrible effect on their lives unless they can get help to overcome them.

Some people have a phobia about **injections**.

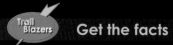

Fear is exciting

We all like to be scared when we know we are safe, or the thing we are frightened of is imaginary.

But some people like to do really scary stuff.

Swimming with sharks.

Mountain climbing.

12

Jumping off mountains.

Isn't this just showing off?

Maybe, but the changes in your brain and body when you are really scared can give you a thrill.

Your brain makes a special 'drug' which makes you feel good. Some people get hooked on being frightened, just as they can get hooked on other drugs.

Bungee jumping.

13

Scary creatures you wouldn't want to meet!

The Mongolian Death Worm

This creature is supposed to live in the **Gobi Desert**. It is a fat, red worm which is between ½ metre and 1½ metres long.

Local people say that it spits out a **yellow poison** which will kill you if it gets onto your flesh.

The Kraken

This is the greatest of all **sea-monsters**. Sailors said it was as big as a small island!

The Kraken wrapped its arms around the ship's hull and pulled it under the water. The sailors would drown and the monster could eat them.

The stories of the Kraken were probably sightings of **giant squid**. Giant squid have been known to attack ships (probably thinking they were whales!)

Scary warnings

You are sitting quietly at home one evening when you hear a dreadful **howling** and **screaming** outside.

Maybe the lady next door has dropped a brick on her foot ... or maybe it's a **banshee**.

In Irish **mythology** the banshee is a ghostly spirit. She wails outside houses where someone is about to die.

In other parts of the world, warnings of death are made by strange **black dogs**. They are usually bigger than a normal dog, and have glowing eyes.

In parts of the U.K. this dog is known as **Black Shuck**.

In 1577 Black Shuck ran into a **church** in the town of **Bungay**.

Some of the people in the church died at the sight of him. Their bodies were **horribly shrivelled**.

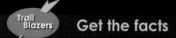

Ghosts

You are in a **strange, old house**.
A door slams behind you ...

You know there is no one else
in the house, but you hear
footsteps, getting closer ...

The room you are in suddenly
goes **freezing cold** ...

You notice a **terrible smell**. It
smells like something that has
been **dead** a long time ...

A damp patch on the wall
looks just like a **face**. Its eyes
open and stare at you ...

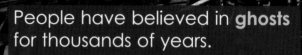
People have believed in **ghosts**
for thousands of years.

So what are they?

- **Spirits** of dead people?

- **Pictures** from the past?

- Sounds and pictures
  made in our own **brain**?

Most ghostly things aren't ghostly at all.

- Spooky sounds and cold spots can be made when the temperature changes..

- People's brains are very good at seeing faces – even when there isn't really a face there!

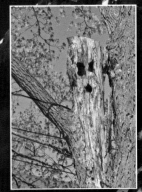

Screaming skulls

A famous screaming skull is hidden somewhere in this house, called **Burton Agnes Hall**.

The house was built by three sisters. One of them was murdered before the house was finished.

When she was buried, **terrible screams** came from her grave. They only stopped when the head was brought back to the house.

The legend says she wanted to see what the finished house was like!

17

Just my Imagination?

A wolf came through my bedroom door

'A wolf came through my bedroom door,
His paws pad-padding on the floor.

I felt his hot breath on my face,
It seemed so real,
It seemed he was really there.

The wolves came through my bedroom wall,
My muscles couldn't move at all.

Their heads were huge,
Red eyes, hungry teeth dribbling,
Great hungry teeth ...

Then I woke up. And that was that.'

So why are there paw prints on your mat?

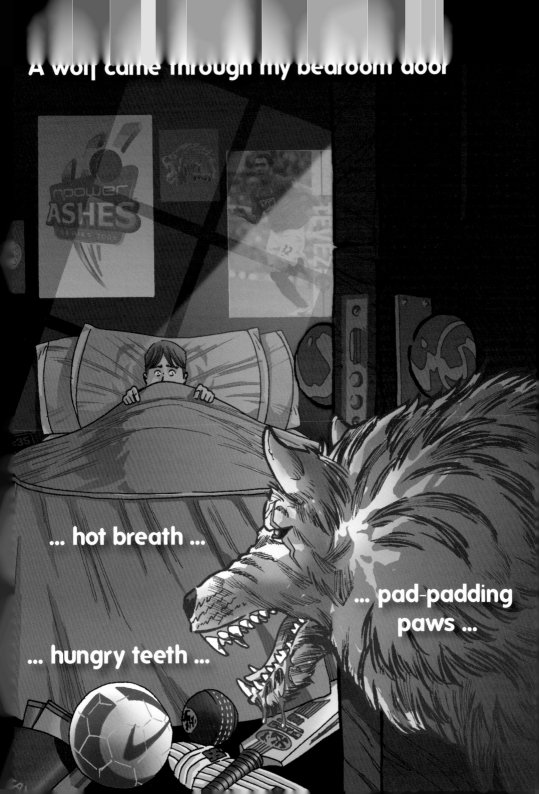

I'd rather not tell

Over the bridge
Across the field
Up the hill
And down the lane.
There's a house in a garden
I visited once.
And I'll never go there again.

A house in a garden,
A room in a house,
A box in a room
Where only the mice
Are awake when
– Now and again –
The lid gently opens,
All by itself,
And out comes – well?
No, I'd rather not tell.

Over the bridge
Across the field
Up the hill
And down the lane.
There's a house in a garden
I visited once.

And I'll never go there again.

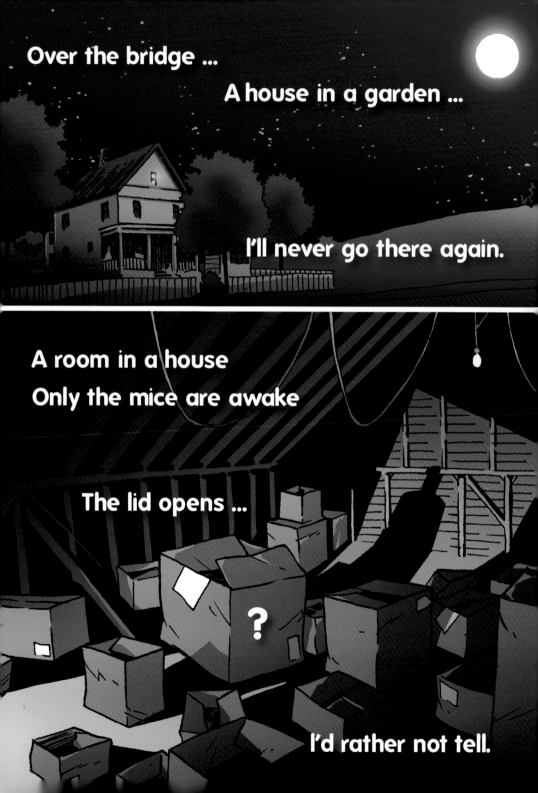

The coal-black hound

When the night is dark
And the mist lies thick
And rats are huddled
In barn and rick.

Beware the eyes
And the teeth and the sound
Of the padding paws
Of the coal-black hound!

Past silent houses
The black hound prowls,
Then he stops at a door
And slobbers and howls:

Those, silent inside, turn grey with fear,
The story's clear: when the black hound speaks,
One in that house
Will be dead in a year.

The young and the newcomers
Laugh at their fear.
'A ghostly hound? Dead in a year?
They're a superstitious lot round here!'

But they remember the tale of the coal-black
     hound
When, within twelve months
That coffin bumps slowly
Into the ground –

And they sit by the fire
When the fog lies thick;
'He was bound to die!
He was old and sick!

'A coal-black hound
With glowing eyes
And the eerie sound
Of padding paws
And mournful howls
And slobbering jaws –

'Believe all that?
What do you take us for?'

But they listen for the sound
Of the hound at the door.

... within
twelve months.

They listen for the sound
of the hound at the door.

Going batty

From our day
We peer into his night world,
And suddenly
It's a late night horror film:

Like Draculas in dirty raincoats,
Zoo bats push and quarrel on their branch,
Jaws aching
For juicy fruit
To throttle and suck dry.

I'm glad there's a wall of glass
Between them and me,
Especially when I look down and see
Orange peel like victims' skin
Shrivelled underneath their tree.

Wanderman

Who are you,
Wanderman?

Lost, maybe,
Lost a life's span.

Your white coat glooms
In the shadows by the church.

Where are the rooms
Of Wanderman?

Take care children
As you hurry past,
Wanderman is fast –

He'll catch you if he can.

Sweet dreams

Do you think of villains, when in bed at night,
And sleep won't come, and noises frighten you?
Do shadows move when you turn out the light?

Do you lie awake and think of things that might
Lurk under beds, and what those things might do?
Do you think of villains, when in bed at night?

There's nothing there at all, you know that's right,
But villains can still scare when they're untrue,
If shadows move, when you've turned out the light.

Do you ever think you might have just caught sight
Of holes in walls, with red eyes staring through?
Do you think of villains, when in bed at night?

Do sudden howling winds give you a fright?
Your curtains flapping at the window, too,
Make shadows move, when you've turned out the
        light.

Do your thoughts keep coming back to things that
        bite,
And lurking strangers in the wardrobe, who
Are surely villains, watching you at night,
Making shadows, turning out your light?

Imagination

There's a horrible thing in the wardrobe,
That comes out when I turn off the light.

There's a thing by my bed
With fingers just waiting,
To tickle my toes in the night.

There's a thing in the garden that
Howls at the moon.

A thing in the hall dark and grim,
'It's just your imagination, that's all,' says Mum.

I don't like the sound of him.

Just your imagination?

Fear word check

anaconda

banshee

Black Shuck

frightened

ghost

giant squid

Gobi desert

hound

imagination

Kraken

money-spider

Mongolian death worm

muscles

mythology

nervous system

phobia

poisonous

prey

shrivelled

skull

superstitious

temperature

unexpected

victim

villain